How to W

Deliver a Eulogy

Practical advice and guidance to support you through a difficult process

David Hartley

Printed Future Ltd.

ISBN paperback: 978-1-7385392-0-8

ISBB e-book: 978-1-7385392-1-5

"Grief is the price we pay for love."

Queen Elizabeth II

Table of Contents

Introduction

Condolences

First of all, sorry for your loss. Nobody buys a book on writing a eulogy for light reading, so if you have lost somebody that is important to you, please accept my sincere condolences. At a time of grief and mourning, this book is designed to ease the process of writing a eulogy during the challenging period before the funeral service.

The contents of this book deal with the essentials of planning, writing and delivering a eulogy, offering practical guidance and simple steps to take away some of the stress of preparing a tribute. Later chapters provide a guided approach on ways to prepare for speaking in public that should prepare you to deliver your words in a way that engages the audience.

Many people worry about speaking in public under normal circumstances, let alone during a gathering to say goodbye to a loved friend or family member. This book offers practical tips on planning ahead to reduce the number of unknowns and potential stresses on the day of the funeral. Setting time aside for preparation will pay dividends in terms of managing nerves, allowing you to focus on saying your own goodbyes and worry less about delivering the eulogy.

Grieving process

The process of researching, writing, practising and finally delivering a Eulogy can provide a positive way to focus feelings of loss and bewilderment during the early stages of grief. The approach this book offers is largely focused on creating a positive celebration of the life that was lived, even if it came to an end too soon. In my experience, reflecting on my father's life and achievements and relaying them back to his friends, colleagues and family provided the first steps on the journey of dealing with his death.

Opportunity to create a lasting tribute

By writing and delivering a eulogy you have a unique opportunity to make a lasting tribute to the person that you have lost. The fact that you have been nominated to deliver the eulogy by either the person that has passed or their family shows you are already trusted to do a good job. Although there is work and perhaps some worry ahead, this book provides guidance on how to make a success of one of the most important tasks you can be entrusted with.

Practical tips from personal experience

I lost my own father to cancer in 2021, as his eldest son I wanted to represent our immediate family and pay tribute to him at the funeral service. Though I occasionally speak in front of large groups in my professional life, I felt some trepidation knowing that I would be in front of a large group of our extended family and his friends and former colleagues. I found there to be very little advice available on the specifics of how to prepare the content, and even less on how to go about creating a solid, engaging delivery. I made notes on what I found to be the hardest parts of the process, with a view to eventually publishing this guide to help people at a time of loss.

During the wake for my father, multiple people come up to me to compliment me on the eulogy, even asking for copies to take away with them. Receiving those kind words gave me great solace that I had done a good job of paying respect to my father, it made the hours spent planning and preparing even more worthwhile.

A long-established tradition

The origin of the word eulogy is in both classical Greek and Latin, and made its way into use in ancient English in the 16th century, literally meaning 'high praise'. The tradition of delivering a short speech in tribute to the deceased has been around for centuries, though there are variations between cultures in when and where during the day it is delivered. This book does not aim to cover the multiple permutations in funeral rituals but does offer guidance on the common options for when and where a eulogy will be given, so you can plan accordingly.

Getting the best from this book

Make notes in the book

This book has been designed to be used as a scribble pad to make notes and jot down your thoughts and ideas as you work through the steps of planning, writing, and practising. Most of the chapters include 'end of chapter prompts' in a tabular format that are designed to be written directly into as you work through the book.

An A4 workbook is available to purchase pre-populated with the end of chapter prompts, entitled 'How to Write and Deliver a Eulogy - Workbook' (ISBN 978-1-7385392-2-2). The workbook has larger spaces for making hand-written notes and additional lined pages for your own thoughts.

No need to follow the sequence of chapters

It may be that you started reading this guide after making a substantial start on writing a eulogy, or that you are more interested in the tips on delivery rather than writing. There is no need to follow a strict order of working through the chapters, just jump to the sections that offer the most immediate advice.

If you are starting to write a eulogy from scratch, the book has been put together in a sequence that puts the items requiring long-term planning at the start of the book, and less time-critical items towards the end. In this case it makes sense to run through from start to finish.

Take it in small steps

Writing a eulogy can feel like a daunting task at the beginning, one of the reasons I wanted to share my experience in this book. My advice is to view the whole task as a series of small checkpoints, each one a step on the way to being complete and ready. Chapters in this book represents useful chunks of progress in your preparation when the prompts and actions have been completed.

Planning: venue, dates and timings

Guidance on order of events

In the United Kingdom it is most likely that a eulogy will be delivered during the funeral service itself. This is true whether it is a religious service in a church, or a civil service in a crematorium or other location. Typically, the eulogy will be delivered in the middle section of the service, so be prepared to relocate from your seat to the front of the venue to deliver the eulogy at the appropriate time. Usually, an Order of Service document is prepared with a running order for the various elements of the service, this will give a good indication of when you need to be ready.

In the United States it is more common for eulogies to be delivered after a religious service, typically during the funeral reception or wake after the service and the committal. There tends to be greater variation of when speeches or the eulogy are delivered, so it is important to fully understand the order of events well in advance of the day of the funeral. If you are not directly involved in defining the running order of the funeral, it would be worth checking with the organiser on when in the running order the eulogy will feature.

In recent years there has been an increased trend for direct funerals, in this case the deceased is buried or cremated very quickly after they pass away. Direct funerals typically consist of a low-key service with minimal or no mourners present. Sometime after the funeral, the family may choose to hold a memorial service, requiring the preparation of a eulogy to commemorate the life of the deceased.

Memorial services may also be held on significant anniversaries relating to the person that passed away, perhaps a significant birthday, or a certain number of years since the anniversary of their death. The eulogy will again typically be in the middle part of any formal memorial ceremony.

Confirm the date and timings

If you aren't already directly involved in the planning of the funeral it is well worth double checking with the organiser that you have the correct date, time and venue for the ceremony. Having the date confirmed early in the process allows you to plan backwards from that point in time, organising the tasks you need to complete to research, write and practise the eulogy.

Understand the venue and practicalities

Later in the book we will cover tips on how to prepare for speaking in public and delivering the eulogy on the day of the funeral. Before this stage there are some key features of the venue that are well worth knowing in advance to allow you to prepare both physically and mentally.

Useful items to know in advance are:

- travel to the venue if you are not part of the funeral cortege, is there a simple way for you to get to the venue in plenty of time?
- accessibility - if you have impaired mobility is the venue simple enough to access? Are there any stairs to the lectern or stage that you need to navigate? If so and you need assistance, is there somebody to guide you?
- audibility - is there a microphone available to use, or will you need to project your voice more than usual?
- rehearsal - is a there a planned run through for the ceremony or a briefing with the person officiating? Will there be chance to practise speaking in the venue in advance?

It will be impossible to second guess every detail of the venue, but establishing the basics in advance will allow you to focus on preparation more fully.

Time limits and constraints

I would strongly recommend getting in touch with the person that will be officiating the service to verify whether there is a maximum time limit that the eulogy needs to be limited to. Some venues run multiple funerals in a day, so a hard time limit needs to be respected in this case. Smaller venues or more remote locations may be less stringent with time limits, or indeed not have any at all.

You should also consider the attention span of the audience; it isn't always easy to listen to a single voice for a long time no matter how hard you try and concentrate. My personal recommendation is to aim for a duration of five to ten minutes. We'll touch more on editing the eulogy to the correct length later in the book, but the priority is to establish any hard time limits before you start detailed preparation.

End of chapter prompts (venue, date and timings)

Prompt	Notes
Date of the funeral	
Time remaining to prepare (days)	
Venue address	
Travel plan	
Who is leading the service?	
When will the eulogy be delivered?	
Time limit (minutes)	

End of chapter prompts (venue, date and timings, continued)

Prompt	Notes
Venue accessibility, any issues to consider?	
Is a rehearsal planned, what date and time?	
Will there be a microphone to use?	
Any additional notes on venue, dates and timings	

Planning: outfit and comfort for speaking

Get an outfit organised early

An area that is often overlooked in getting ready for speaking in public is making sure that you will be physically comfortable when you are addressing the audience. Getting organised early with an outfit for the funeral, and some provisions for preserving my voice, gave me an early sense of achievement and took some of the stress out of the day itself.

Make sure your outfit is comfortable for speaking

If you don't often wear formal clothing, putting on a smart shirt or blouse for the first time in a while could result in a tight fit around the neck. Double check that your outfit for the day allows you to breathe fully and isn't too restrictive. You'll be able to speak more freely in an outfit that fits comfortably. Getting the fit checked early in the planning process will give you time to order a new shirt or make adjustments should you need them.

Practical footwear

If you need to walk any distance at the funeral or climb any stairs in the venue to deliver the eulogy, make sure that you have suitable footwear to avoid trips or slips. Leather soles or high heels look very smart but may not be practical, especially if the weather is forecast to be poor. You may need to purchase some smart, practical footwear to complement your chosen outfit.

Take the pressure off your voice

It's worth thinking through what you may need on the day to make sure that your voice can last through delivering the eulogy. To prevent coughing or a dry throat a throat lozenge could be useful, as would a bottle of water (or access to a drink just before you speak). Think about whether you need to ask a friend or family member to bring these items along for you if you won't have a bag with you on the day.

Check the final appearance of your outfit

If you are wearing an outfit with pockets, avoid the temptation to fill them excessively to avoid bulges and bumps that can detract from you looking your absolute best. Having keys, packets of lozenges etc in a pocket can also result in an irresistible temptation to fiddle with them while you are speaking, which can be distracting for the audience.

I am always guilty of carrying my mobile phone in my inside jacket pocket, both ruining the line of my suit and creating the risk of it going off when I am speaking. If you can safely leave your phone, wallet and keys with a friend or family member during the service it would be worth doing so. Worrying about where to stash all these useful props and possessions is perhaps less of an issue for those that carry a handbag!

The aim is to let your outfit hang on you as smoothly as possible, creating the best possible impression when you stand up to speak.

How will you carry essentials for the service?

Although you don't want to ruin the line of your outfit, you will need to carry your speaking notes or script to the lectern, and possibly reading glasses if you need them. If you don't wear your funeral outfit often, consider where you will store these key items on your person so that you can access them quickly and easily. It may be the best plan of action to purchase a small portfolio case or smart folder to keep everything neat and tidy.

End of chapter prompts (outfit and comfort for speaking)

Prompt	Notes
List any new clothing items you need to purchase for the day, including footwear	
Have you checked whether existing clothes fit well?	
Can you sit and breathe comfortably in your chosen outfit?	
Do you need anything to support your voice? Water, lozenges etc.	
Where will you keep tissues or a handkerchief?	
Where will you keep your glasses, phone etc on the day?	
Whereabouts on your person will your keep a written copy of the eulogy?	
Do you need a folder or portfolio case to help carry the script flat?	

Planning: blocking out time to prepare

Make dedicated time slots to plan, write and practise

The death of a loved one creates a massive number of tasks that need to be dealt with in the immediate aftermath. From letting friends and family know what has happened to rearranging your own personal and work commitments, the list grows quickly. You may need to assist with organising the funeral service and start to plan for what will happen to the deceased's estate. Dealing with raw grief and emotions as well as a large task list can at times be overwhelming. Add the pressure of writing and delivering a eulogy into the mix and it can be difficult to know how to make a start.

I found the key to making life easier for myself was to plan specific blocks of time for researching, writing, editing, and practising the eulogy. Blocking one or two hour slots (or even longer if you have the time available) and dedicating them to the eulogy task allows tangible progress to be made in each session. Knowing that you have time dedicated in your diary should mean there is one less thing to worry about.

It may be worth planning the time slots around when you are able to focus fully - is there a quieter time when you will have a room or the house to yourself to work without distractions? If your home environment is busy, it could be worth finding somewhere that you can work alone, perhaps a local library or cafe. Everybody has a different style of focusing and working, so play to your own strengths and try to avoid leaving everything to the last minute to get the best result.

Key tasks to set time aside for

When planning out the time you need to spend on the Eulogy, there are four key areas that need to have time set aside.

1. Research and gathering content ideas

2. Creating a structure and writing the content detail

3. Practising delivering the eulogy

4. Refining the words and delivery

Approximate time allocation

There is no definitive amount of time to spend on each element of preparing the content. Everybody's personal circumstances on how much time they can set aside to prepare before the funeral will be different for a myriad of reasons. The practicalities of keeping life going for your household, work commitments, and the amount of time between the death and the funeral will be different for everyone.

The best guidance that I can give is that for the time that I had available I spent roughly the following proportion of my planned time on each task:

- 30% on research and content gathering
- 50% on structuring and writing the content
- 15% on practising the delivery
- 5% on refining the words and delivery

These allocations are approximate and will vary depending on your personal style of working and to what extent you are a confident public speaker. If you are really pressed for time, the last two can be omitted completely, but I would recommend against it.

What is most important is to block time out in your diary, and when you do allocate time make sure you are free of distractions so that you can fully focus on the task in hand.

End of chapter prompts (making time to prepare)

Prompt	Notes
Have you blocked out time slots in your diary for preparing the eulogy? When is this time?	
Can you find a place to work that will be productive?	
For the time you have available, split the time into research, writing, practising and refining.	
What steps can you take to minimise distraction in the time you have blocked?	

Gather the content: where to look

Create a list of places to research

Finding the content to include in a eulogy can seem like a mountain to climb, but it is surprising how quickly a short list of facts, stories and reminiscences can turn into a list of topics to include in a finished product. In this chapter we'll cover good ways to capture ideas for content, in the next chapter we'll talk about organising them into structured story.

It's important to remember the maximum time limit of ten minutes length, anything longer and you may struggle to hold the audience's attention. A time limit also creates a useful way of cutting down content and making sure that you stay focused on the most important details that need to be covered. If you break down the ten minutes, each story or anecdote lasting a couple of minutes will soon fill up the time.

Think about who will be attending

The guest list for the funeral could be a good source of ideas for the opening of the eulogy. Is anyone is making a special effort to attend the funeral? Will they be flying in from another country or travelling a long distance to be at the service on the day. If so, this can be a useful way to open the eulogy by thanking people for their effort to attend. Once the guest list has been confirmed it's a simple list to write out and gives you an easy way to start speaking without getting too nervous.

Did the deceased leave any details?

It may be that the person you have lost gave some detail on how they would like to be remembered on the day of their funeral (my father certainly had some very clear ideas on what he wanted to be said about his hiking achievements, he was very proud of what he had accomplished). That guidance can be invaluable and makes a great starting point for content to include. Unfortunately, many people pass away suddenly or unexpectedly, so this is by no means a guaranteed way of getting content ideas.

Ask friends and family for favourite anecdotes, look at sympathy cards

There is no need to come up with all of the ideas for the eulogy yourself, talk to friends and family about their memories of the deceased. There will be so many anecdotes and stories people mention that ideas will start to flow - you may even learn something about the deceased that you weren't aware of.

My father was a teacher, though he taught humanities he was extremely sporty and was often involved in Physical Education lessons and supporting the school sport teams. One of his oldest teaching friends wrote a lovely card to the family reminiscing about a staff versus student football game that he and my dad played together in. They had worked out that the four players in the back row of the defence had a combined age of over 200 years (and they still beat the students!)

The story made me smile during a time of loss, I felt grateful that the friend had taken the time to share a fond memory of my father. I used the story virtually word for word in the eulogy.

Trust your own recollections and instincts

If you have been given the responsibility of writing the eulogy, then don't shy away from including your own personal memories and stories in the content. Make a list of three favourite anecdotes or memories that you look back on fondly. You don't need to write them out in full at this point, just jot down some quick headlines that can be expanded on later in the process. One of my favourite childhood memories of my father was witnessing the almightiest explosion of his home-brew beer all over a brand-new kitchen in the family home. A simple, silly story that raised a smile and captured several of his personality traits (food and drink lover, industrious and accident prone!)

Family history / photograph archives

Photograph albums or collections of digital pictures are a great way of looking back on the most significant parts of somebody's life story. Before the advent of digital cameras, film cameras usually only came out at significant events or when something of note was happening. If you have access to the deceased's family photographs, flicking through these will generate some good ideas of events and topics to include in the eulogy. Examples could include favourite holidays and trips, meeting interesting people, family events, passions, and hobbies worthy of mention.

When adding more detail later, you may be able to use the photographs to verify timelines of significant events in the family history or the deceased's career.

If you are lucky enough to have somebody interested in genealogy in the family, this can be a treasure trove of detail for timelines of births, marriages, and significant life events. Even without a written history, there is often somebody in a family who has an encyclopaedic knowledge of what happened when to each of the family members. Reach out to them to firm up the facts on any key dates and events that you are considering including.

Social media research

Social media apps can be a great help in finding ideas for topic contents to include in a eulogy, and some of them have been around for longer than you may think. Using LinkedIn can be helpful to check on the details of the deceased's career, showing exactly where they used to work with a timeline. LinkedIn has been around since 2003, but often users include details of their early career, qualifications and sometimes even details of their education. Facebook and Twitter (or X more recently) have both been around since 2006, so if the deceased was an early adopter there is a potentially large repository of memories and photographs to look back and generate topic ideas from. Instagram came along 2010 and can provide a rich source of photographs covering favourite places, events, holidays, people etc.

End of chapter prompts (where to gather content)

Create a list of the best areas to research content ideas. If you are short of time, prioritise the areas you will look at first to get the most valuable content. The list can include key people to talk to for advice and inspiration.

Prompt	Places to research
Place 1	
Place 2	
Place 3	
Place 4	
Place 5	
Place 6	
Place 7	
Place 8	

Gather the content: create topic ideas

Initial list of topics

I found the most useful way to start creating the content was to make a list subject areas or topics that I wanted to include in the eulogy. Using this list of topics as building blocks will create some initial structure before writing in more detail. The outline structure provides focus on where you will need to do further research if required in the latter stages of writing. The following section of this chapter provide ideas for topics to include the eulogy.

Opening thanks and apologies

Even if there are no guests from far-flung places, it's worth jotting down a quick couple of sentences on how you would like to thank everyone that has taken time out to pay respect to the deceased. If somebody was desperate to attend the funeral but was unable to (perhaps through illness or frailty) they will inevitably be grateful of a mention on the day itself, especially if the eulogy is being recorded or streamed for them.

Thanks to the person officiating the service

You may wish to publicly offer thanks to the person that is officiating the extended funeral service on behalf of yourself and the family, particularly if they were well known to the deceased. If you don't know them well it's perfectly fine to leave this out, you can always thank them in person after the service.

Reflection on the surroundings

Is the funeral taking place somewhere that was special to the deceased? If it is being held in a religious building, did they attend regularly, or have other family events been held there? A memorial service in particular could be held in any number of unusual locations, so it can be worth mentioning the reason you gathered in the chosen venue to celebrate the life of the deceased.

Create a timeline of key life events

Most eulogies contain a timeline of the deceased's life, career and significant achievements. We'll talk more about structure and ordering in later chapters, but it in terms of researching the content this may be one of the more time-consuming areas to work on. You don't need to go into detail, but it would be worth considering some or all of the following events if they apply:

- Date and place of birth
- Schooling
- University or further education
- First job
- Career highlights
- Did they marry? When / were / how did they meet their partner?
- When did they marry, how long were they married for?
- Did they have any children, when were they born?
- Any periods where they lived abroad or significant moves?
- Did they retire? If so, when?

Passions and hobbies

It's always worth touching on the activities that meant the most to the person you are writing about. If they had a hobby that involved a club or a group activity, the chances are that some of those people will be in the audience so a mention will be warmly received. Perhaps there were some hobbies that were more private that may surprise people, did they paint or write and not everybody knew about it? Was there a favourite sports team that they followed fervently? Were they a collector? Did they love travel and the outdoors? Was music an inspiration in their life? Highlighting their hobbies and why they were so passionate about them is a good way to get a solid paragraph of the speech written and make some early progress

Career or professional highlights

Work often forms a major part of somebody's life, and sometimes forms a major part of their identity. A quick summary of the deceased's career and achievements is always worth including in the eulogy. If you don't have the exact details of where they worked and when, reaching out to former colleagues is a good way to fill in the details and may provide some additional insight. You may get a different perspective of how they were perceived in the workplace compared to home life.

Personal achievements and awards

If the person that you have lost made any exceptional achievements during their lifetime, it is well worth doing some research about what made them so special and why they received the award. If they were in the forces or worked in the public sector, perhaps they were honoured for their service in some way? If they were academic or worked in a scientific capacity, did they win any prizes for their work that are worth mentioning? Were there any sporting or physical achievements that would be interesting to mention? My own father was a keen cricketer and lawn bowls player, so I made sure to mention the teams he played for.

Contributions to charity, community, family etc.

Did the deceased make an exceptional contribution to somebody's upbringing in the family or help somebody elderly in their neighbourhood. Did they serve their community in another way, perhaps through volunteering or helping at a community or sports group? Perhaps they received an award or formal acknowledgement of the service that they gave. There may be several noteworthy achievements that can be grouped together into this topic.

Anecdotes and stories

Finding the strength to include amusing anecdotes in a eulogy isn't always easy, but it is often the amusing stories about a person that are the most memorable and the easiest to retell. I found thinking back over funny memories of my father helped to lighten my mood during a tough time, they were the easiest sections of the eulogy to write and help me feel as though I was starting to make tangible progress.

A story that lightens the mood a little on the day is worth considering, whether it be a funny misunderstanding, an amusing culinary disaster or something more slapstick. Stories from within the close family circle are often worth mentioning as not all of the audience members will have heard them before.

Or course, not all stories in the eulogy need to be funny, if there are some interesting or quirky tales about the deceased that would be of interest to the audience make a note of them as topics. Give each anecdote a short title so that you can structure and reorder them later in the writing process.

How will life be different / harder going forward?

Making some notes about how you will be affected by the loss of the deceased is time well invested. If you choose to include some words on this subject, then remember that it is something very personal to you and it could be hard to speak about on the day of the funeral. You could include something simple like missing a daily phone call, or something more serious like a reflection on aspects of your family's life that won't be the same anymore. Jot down a few ideas and expand on this later, it can be hard to get the words exactly right for this topic and may need a little soul searching on how the death will really impact you.

What was their legacy / lasting impact?

Make some notes about any lasting impact the deceased has had on you and your family. Have they instilled a love of a certain hobby or sport? Have they instilled a work ethic or sense of humour that you will forever be grateful for? Did they influence your life and decisions in a positive way that you can mention and share thanks for? This can be a useful way to close out the eulogy and say a lasting thank you in front of a public audience.

Any last wishes or fresh starts?

Did the deceased ask you to raise a toast in their memory, or to make sure that you took a holiday to a special destination in their memory. Have they inspired you to do something new or live in the moment now they have gone? If so, share what you'll do in their memory.

End of chapter prompts (create topic ideas)

Create some initial bullet points of the topics you want to include in the eulogy. Go for a longer list to start with, it's easier to edit down than be stuck for ideas when time is short.

Prompt	Topic titles
Opening thanks and apologies	
Timeline of key life events for inclusion	
Summary of passions and hobbies	

End of chapter prompts (create topic ideas, continued)

Prompt	Topic titles
Career / professional highlights	
Achievements and awards	
Contributions to community, charity etc.	

End of chapter prompts (create topic ideas, continued)

Prompt	Topic titles
Favourite funny anecdotes	
How will they be missed	
Did they leave a legacy behind?	

End of chapter prompts (create topic ideas, continued)

Prompt	Topic titles
Last wishes or fresh starts	
Any other ideas	

Write the content: dos and don'ts

Create a list of dos and don'ts

Soon we'll start to organise our topics into a structure that will provide the framework to expand the text into a completed eulogy. Let's start with some basic dos and don'ts to start with to avoid heading down any false avenues and hopefully minimising future editing work. If there are any tips from the following list that resonate with you, make a note of them in the end-of-chapter prompts before you start writing.

Dos

- Remember your audience will be varied. Try and include key groups that will be there on the day (for example, mention something to do with their career if former colleagues will be present).

- Be selective. There isn't time to include every detail, start with a longer list of topics and trim it down if you need to later.

- Use the positive support of friends and family to help with the writing process. A collaboration is perfectly acceptable for preparing the content of the eulogy. If someone has provided stories, give them a mention - they will appreciate that you valued their input and gave them public thanks.

- Try and use a story or narrative approach rather than bullet points or lists. It's fine to make bullets for prompts or initial thoughts but be careful not to read out lists during the eulogy as it can be perceived as impersonal. Using a story-based, narrative approach is easier to listen too for the audience.

- Make sure that you have the equipment to get you started on writing, either plenty of paper and ink or a well-charged laptop.

Don'ts

- Try and to use words that aren’t your natural way of speaking. Writing out stories in your natural speaking style will make it easier to deliver on the day. Beware over reliance on AI text generation tools for this reason.

- Go into too much detail on the cause of death. If they battled bravely through a long disease, then of course mention this if you want to. Don’t go into too much detail on the finer points of exactly how they died, it can be upsetting for people in the audience.

- Settle scores, either with the deceased or with family and friends present. Words said in the height of emotion are difficult to retract. Focus on the positives of the person you have lost.

- Mention family disputes. It's hard enough bringing people with deep-seated disagreements into the same room, so it's best not to go into any detail if the deceased was in some way involved in a family dispute.

- Be too shocking or risqué. There will probably be multiple generations present at the funeral, including elderly and young people present who could potentially be offended. It's best to moderate the tone of your stories to exclude any very colourful or illegal stories about the deceased, especially if the venue is inside a church. You can always write out anything that you weren't sure about including for discussion in a more private setting.

End of chapter prompts (content dos and don’ts)

Prompt	Notes
List out any of the dos and don'ts that resonate with you before you start writing in detail	

Write the content: create an outline structure

Ordering topics into a structure

Hopefully by now you should have a list of stories or topics that you want to cover in the eulogy, and a list of any dos and don'ts or reminders that you want to remember throughout the writing process. The first task is to structure the topics into a logical order so that the eulogy flows smoothly from beginning to end. It can help to write the topics onto scraps of paper so that you can shuffle and re-order them. If you are working electronically use a brief description of each topic that you can cut and paste into the final outline structure.

Basic structure: beginning, middle and end

Every speech (even if it isn't a eulogy) needs a beginning, a middle and an end. Group your topics together, linking similar items together into themes, you can then decide on a rough initial order to arrange them into.

The beginning

Topics that sit logically at the start of the eulogy may include:

- Welcome and thanks
- Special mentions and apologies from those absent
- Reflection on the surroundings, weather etc
- Timeline of the deceased's life events

The middle: group into themes

Topics that fit logically into the middle of the eulogy may include:

- Passions and hobbies
- Career or professional highlights
- Personal achievements or awards
- Contributions to charity, community etc
- Anecdotes and stories

To structure the middle section of the eulogy, take an objective look at the topics you have listed out - are there any common themes that emerge? My father was quite accident prone, a running joke in the family - lots of our favourite family stories and memories of him revolve around domestic disasters that he was involved in. Perhaps work ethic, or other personality traits emerge, or favourite sports, hobbies, locations could be consistently cropping up. Identifying and grouping stories into themes provides useful threads that can weave the middle section of the eulogy together nicely.

The middle: chronological order can work well

If there aren't any obvious themes emerging that would provide structure, that doesn't need to be a problem. Sticking with a chronological order makes plenty of sense and provides a useful way of organising stories you want to include. If the list of topics starts with stories from the deceased's childhood or school days, start with those and work forward in sequence until the most recent.

The end

Heads up - this is the hardest section to write and the hardest to deliver on the day. It's here that you want to sum up what the deceased meant to you, their friends and family. You can cover how you will miss them and the legacy they have left behind. It's worth considering breaking the end of the eulogy down into small sections that are easy to write in smaller sessions.

Topics that logically fit into the closing stages of the eulogy may include:

- How will life be different / harder going forward?
- What was their legacy / lasting impact?
- Any last wishes or fresh starts?"

Expanding sections or themes

Once the structure is complete, writing out each of the individual sections doesn't seem too daunting (rather than attempting to write the whole thing from scratch). I found that this approach allowed me to focus in short bursts, completing one or two sections in a sitting, and giving me time to think ahead on the upcoming parts. We'll cover this in detail in the next chapter.

End of chapter prompts (create an outline structure)

Prompt	Notes
Choose how you will structure the topics that you want to cover (themes, timeline etc)	
Create the outline structure in the order that you will deliver it on the day of the funeral	
Take a picture or save an electronic copy so your work isn't lost	

Write the content: add the detail

Expand the topic headings

It's time to expand each of the stories and topics that you have selected and carefully structured. Start writing out in full one of the topics that you would most easily recount to a friend or family member (perhaps a funny memory of the deceased that you have chosen to include) and go from there. It's helpful to make some good solid progress early on to give you a feeling of getting the task completed. There's no need to start at the beginning and work your way through to the end.

Write as it comes to you

Capture your thoughts as they come to you and get them down on the paper (or screen) without analysing too much initially. It's easier to chop and edit a draft script, rather than worrying about the fact that you need to write it in the first place. Don't worry about spelling and grammar checks to start with, just get the words down in a rough format.

Complete your research

If there are topics that need more detailed research (for example dates and locations relating to major life events that you want to cover), now is the time to complete the research fully. It's still possible to start writing out the topics that need researching, just leave places to insert the missing dates/place etc that you are researching and add them later on.

Keep a note pad handy

I found that once I had started writing out the eulogy, details of what I wanted to say would come to me when I wasn't focusing on the task (on a train journey or taking a shower in the morning). It's worth keeping a notepad to hand so that you can jot down any little gems that come to you during the day.

Ask for help if you need it

Writing the closing of the eulogy can be tough on the emotions. It can be helpful to reach out to friends and family to understand how they are feeling, and what they will miss about the deceased. Nobody will think any less of you if you ask for assistance, the people that you ask may appreciate the opportunity to provide some input into the eulogy.

Put it to one side if you can't make progress

If there is a particular topic that you are struggling to write for whatever reason, put it to one side and come back to it. I found it better to make progress on other sections rather than struggling with one that felt more difficult to complete. You will hopefully find that inspiration comes to you later in the process.

Use AI tools if you want to, but treat with caution

There are many AI writing tools available on the internet. They may be of assistance to you, but I would advise using them with caution. They won't capture your natural style of delivery, and after the event you may feel that you haven't given your best effort on paying your respects to the deceased if you have relied heavily on an AI tool. That's not to say there isn't value in using these tools for editing and checking, but my advice would be to use them with discretion rather than as the default.

Create a checklist of topics to check progress

It is always pleasing to see when you are making progress towards completing a major task. I found creating a list of the topics to be completed, then ticking them off when I had written them fully was a useful motivator. You can also use the list to plan what you need to cover in any remaining time slots that you have set aside for writing.

Make a backup copy when you are finished

Once you have completed the initial draft script of the eulogy, you are well on the way to a finished product. I would recommend making a copy of the draft at this point so that all your hard work isn't lost should anything happen to your notepad or electronic device.

For electronic versions, save a copy to cloud storage or a USB stick, or email it to yourself. For hard copy drafts in notepads or on paper, take some photographs or a photocopy to give yourself peace of mind.

Having a couple of physical copies to hand will also be handy for the editing process. You can get the red pen out without fear of damaging the original notes. We'll go into further detail on editing in the next chapter.

End of chapter prompts (add the detail)

Prompt	Notes
Create a checklist of the topic headings, and mark them as complete as you progress	
List out who you may need to help you on the detail of specific topics	
Backup – have you made physical and/or electronic backup copies of your draft eulogy?	

Write the content: make a copy for editing

Get access to a printer if possible

Editing and practising the eulogy should hopefully be a simpler task than writing out the first full draft. It will be important to have a hard copy so that you can make edits quickly and add annotations about the style of your delivery (which we'll cover in a later chapter). I would expect to print and reprint the eulogy a handful of times as you work through edits and style adaptions.

Writing out in full, or opt for prompt cards

The main decision before starting printing and editing is how you want to read and deliver the eulogy on the day. The main choices are to opt for prompt cards that outline the main points to cover in bullets, or to write the text out in a full script. Each approach has pros and cons, but before preparing the printed material to bring with you on the day you need to choose which way will work best for you.

Using note cards:

Pros

- Quicker to write and edit
- Can make for a more natural speaking style if you are confident working from prompts
- Easy to look around the room and project your voice

Cons

- Creates the potential for extra pressure on the day and missing the exact detail you wanted to cover
- Can't easily be transferred to another person if you are overcome with emotion or sick on the day of the funeral
- Greater risk of mixing up cards and losing the flow
- Not as helpful as a lasting written memorial, can't be sent on to people that were unable to attend the funeral

Fully written script:

Pros

- Reduces pressure on the day, everything you need to say is fully written out
- Can be given to the person officiating the service or a family member as a backup reader
- Copies can be sent on to people unable to attend the funeral
- Easy to practise and perfect the delivery

Cons

- Slightly more cumbersome to carry and lay flat on the lectern
- Can result in a less interesting speaking style without a conscious effort
- More work to edit and finesse the final version

Go with your personal preference

At nearly all the funerals that I have attended, the person delivering the eulogy has chosen to write out their script in full. It comes down to personal preference, but the factors around removing an extra layer of stress and mental gymnastics on the day steered me towards writing out the text in full (even though my usual preference for a speech or presentation would be a few short bullets).

Having the additional backup of a spare eulogy script with the minister on the day of my father's funeral was reassuring. Thankfully I didn't need that support from the minister on the day, and was able to rely on the practise I had put in beforehand to make it through.

The remainder of the sections relating to editing in this book relate to writing out the text in full, and creating a version that is finessed for reading aloud.

Use topics as sub-headings initially

During the first phases of editing, you may find that you want to chop around or move sections of the text. Re-structuring text is much easier if you keep the initial topic names as headers for each main section. You can choose whether to add or delete the headings as you get close to the final version of the text, I left them in my eulogy script as useful reminders to take a deep breath.

Example eulogy

The appendix of this book contains the eulogy that I wrote for my own father Roger. You can see the topic headings that I used to structure and edit the script. The topics are extremely specific to my own dear Dad, but the approach should apply to whoever you need to write for.

The example eulogy has been included to provide guidance and to show that the task ahead isn't insurmountable. I certainly do not claim it to be an exemplar and would advise against using it as a direct template for your own tribute.

End of chapter prompts (make a copy for editing)

Prompt	Notes
Choose whether to use note cards or a written script	
Structure your text with topic headings to allow easier editing	
Create a first hard copy that can be used for editing and annotations	

Edit the content: polish the final version

First read, roughly how long is it?

The first job is to check approximately how long it will take to read out the full draft. Using a timer, read the whole eulogy at your natural speaking pace. It is worth reading aloud to get some early practise in advance of the day of the funeral. Unless you do a lot of speaking in public, you will probably need to speak a little more slowly and clearly than you expect to make yourself audible and understandable. Don't rush through reading out the draft when you make the first timing, slower is better.

A good way to get an approximate estimation of the duration of you content is to use the 'read aloud' function in your word processing software. You can time how long it takes the software to work through the text, the reading speed is roughly what you should be aiming for to create good audibility when speaking in front of an audience.

Don't be cautious with the red pen

If there is no time limit for the eulogy I would recommend ten minutes as a maximum, both to preserve your voice and keep the attention of those listening. If the eulogy is way too long on the first read, then it's best to take decisive action and cut out some whole topics if necessary.

It will never be possible to say everything that you want to about the deceased in a limited time. If you do find that you are chopping large sections out, save the work that you have done in case you are inspired later to put together a written memorial or even a photo book. The work you have done won't be wasted.

Use spell and grammar checks

It's worth running the spelling and grammar functions in your word processing software to help capture any basic errors in the script. Getting rid of typos and duplicated words will help you to read it as smoothly as possible when the time comes. The one thing spell checks frequently miss is the use of a stray word that is spelt correctly (e.g. hold instead of gold). Using the 'read aloud' function and listening back to the text can help spot these errors.

Hard to say sections / tongue twisters

After you have edited down the script to a suitable duration, focus on any areas that you found tricky to read out aloud. Look out for the following problems that may derail your delivery:

- Tongue-twisters that are difficult to read out
- Words that you found difficult to pronounce
- Very long sentences where you struggled for breath

If you are caught out by any of the above, make edits to the text to make reading aloud easier. This careful editing will pay dividends in terms of your confidence to speak in front of the people attending the funeral.

Anything too emotional

If there is anything in your draft that is making you upset as you read it aloud, take time to reflect on the best way to edit around this. You don't want to be overcome by emotion, but at the same time if the message is important, it may be best to leave it in. There is no problem with visibly showing your emotions but try to be confident that you will be able to continue to the end.

For any difficult sections, think about the following approaches:

1. Leave it in. Practise reading it aloud or to a family member or friend several times so that it becomes less difficult with repetition
2. Tone down the language. Keep the sentiment but perhaps use some less personal wording so that you can still convey the message
3. Remove the difficult section. There's no shame in making sure that the eulogy goes smoothly on the day.

Take time out to celebrate a major milestone

After this first round of editing, you are most of the way to having your script ready for the funeral. Refining the physical aspects of delivery still needs to be considered, but you have completed by far the greatest part of the work at this point. Every extra piece of effort that you add from now is polishing and preparation that will make the process of giving the eulogy less difficult. Even if you have no more preparation time, you have done the work to commemorate and celebrate the life of the person that you lost.

Make another copy, keep it somewhere safe

The worst possible thing that could happen at this stage is to lose all the work that you have completed. Take another copy of the script and make sure it is physically separated from the original, just in case of a disaster. It's better to be over cautious at this point, it would be a dreadful to lose your hard work.

End of chapter prompts (polish the final version)

Prompt	Notes
Write down the end-to-end duration in minutes, reading aloud steadily	
Tackle any tongue twisters, rephrase if necessary	
Edit or practise sections that are emotionally difficult to read aloud	
Celebrate the milestone of finishing the writing and editing, what will you do?	
Make a backup copy of the finished product. Save it in a different physical location to the original. Remind yourself of the location here	

Finalise the content: prepare the script or cards

Electronic or hard copy

I recommend reading from a hard copy of the eulogy script on the day of the funeral. Relying on an electronic device such as an iPad or a laptop will add an extra layer of uncertainty into the day, adding risk in terms of battery life, screen visibility or total software meltdown. A clearly printed script or card set is simple to work with and easy to carry. Either handwritten or printed is fine, so long as it is legible and clear.

If you are opting for a hand-written version, I would recommend writing it out for a final time after the practising process to minimise the number of strikethroughs, scribbles and markups that could be confusing when reading aloud. For a printed version, make sure that you use a clear font and print it in a sufficiently large size that you can read it clearly.

Make a duplicate script to bring

The most important thing on the day of the funeral is to make sure that you have remembered to bring along a copy of the eulogy that you have carefully prepared. We'll run through the printing / writing out of the finished article, but it is worth making more than one copy that you can give to somebody else who will be attending on the day, just in case you manage to mislay your copy. Try to remember to ask them in advance if they would be willing to hold a backup for you on the day of the funeral.

Where will you keep it on the day?

Think about how you will transport the hard copy to stop it from becoming damaged. If you are using A4 or US Letter size paper, do you need to think about how you will prevent it from becoming crumpled? Ideally the paper will lie as flat as possible on the lectern, or if you are standing in an open space, it should look smart as you hold it up.

If you are planning to carry the copy inside a jacket or blazer, think about how you will need to fold the document to make sure it fits inside a pocket. It may be better to bring a smart folder or portfolio case to hold the script flat.

Note cards are easier to fit in bags and pockets but are harder to handle on the day. If you are using note cards, take the precaution of numbering them just in case you drop them and need to quickly re-order them.

End of chapter prompts (prepare a hard copy)

Prompt	Notes
Make a hard copy and a backup, make sure it is clear and legible	
Nominate somebody to bring a duplicate copy of your eulogy on the day of your funeral	
Think about how to store and transport the copy without damaging it	
If using note cards, number them prominently	

Delivery: practise time

Plan time to practise

Now you have an edited version of the eulogy and a hard copy to read from, the last piece of the puzzle is to practise reading it aloud as much as you can. Setting time aside for practise is a great way to settle nerves, especially if you don't often address a large number of people in your day-to-day life. Practising reading aloud is so much more helpful than reading to yourself at this point, and helps in the following ways:

- Getting used to holding and working with the script
- Reducing your reliance on having to study every word of the script, delivery style becomes more natural
- Working out where breaths and pauses are required
- Getting used to the sensation of reading out any sections that are emotionally difficult

Find a private space to begin with

Take the pressure off yourself at the start of your practise by finding a private space to do the first few read throughs. You can make any basic mistakes and get into the rhythm on your own without anyone watching. This might also be the point for some further adjustments to the script or note cards, you can mark them up and reprint if needed during this phase.

Consider making a recording

If you are feeling brave you could consider making a recording of yourself reading the eulogy. Recordings can make you feel self-conscious, but they are an effective way to find and make improvements. We'll touch on ways to make your speaking voice interesting and audible in the next chapter.

As well as a voice recording you could also consider making a video of yourself reading. We'll cover the physical aspects of delivery later on the book, so hang onto your video clips.

Read in front of somebody

Once you can comfortably get through the eulogy from start to finish without making any major mistakes or stumbles, it is worth asking a close friend or family member to listen.

I found reading the eulogy aloud to my mum on a one-to-one basis was harder than doing it on the day of the funeral, so this is a good confidence builder. She provided some useful feedback on a couple of sections, no doubt using her years of experience as a teacher and speaking to hundreds of kids at once in the assembly hall.

Try to be open to receiving and acting on feedback even though you may have already spent hours on the script by this point. Reading out loud to somebody is a true test of how quickly or slowly you need to cover the text, so it's worth checking the timing for a final time at this point.

Don't over think it

The main point of practising reading aloud is to give yourself more confidence on the day of the funeral, creating familiarity with the content and some muscle memory in terms of speaking aloud and pausing for breath. Nobody is expecting you to deliver a syllable-perfect performance on the day, so don't put yourself under pressure to get everything exactly right. You will have the support of everybody in the room that is suffering from the same sense of loss as you, nobody will judge harshly.

End of chapter prompts (delivery: make time to practise)

Prompt	Notes
Identify a suitable practise space	
Schedule some practise time into your diary	
Find a simple way to make a recording	
Ask someone to listen and give feedback	
Note any feedback from family and friends, then incorporate into the script	

Delivery: speaking style tips

Make some simple improvements

Nobody is expecting you to give an Oscar-winning performance, but there are some basic tips and techniques that can help transform a stumbling, quiet reading into one that everybody can hear and engage with. In my working life I have learned some valuable tools and tricks that make my presentations a little more bearable for the recipients. The same techniques apply to any speaking engagement in front of a large audience. In this chapter I have outlined the techniques that have helped the most over the years.

It would be worth trying to incorporate these tips into your final practise sessions, giving you experience of using them before the day of the funeral. A recording can help massively here, or ask the person you are practising with for some feedback on delivery style.

Be heard

Perhaps the most important tip of them all is to project your voice. You need to make sure that everybody in the room will be able to hear you on the day. The easiest way to do this is to look up at the audience and project your voice to the person sitting in the last row of the venue. In a large building this will require you to speak much more loudly than when you were practising at home.

To remember that you will need to project your voice, make a note on your script to address the first line to the back of the room. A microphone may be a great help here, but you shouldn't rely on technology to help with this – lift your eyes and project your voice.

Being familiar with the script from multiple practise sessions will massively increase your confidence to look up from the script without fear of losing your place.

Go slower than you think is necessary

Inevitably your heart rate and stress level will be elevated when you to stand up and read the eulogy. Increased adrenaline and a certain amount of wanting to get the whole process over with as soon as possible can result in galloping through the words at a pace that is too quick to be audible. If there are older family members and friends in the audience, think of how you would speak to them under normal circumstances. Slow down your talking speed and focus on clear diction to get your message across audibly.

Be the Alps, not Holland

One of the biggest struggles I have to overcome when speaking in public is creating some light and shade in the tone of my voice. Using higher and lower tones to create interest takes some practise, it comes more naturally to some than others. Essentially you trying to avoid speaking in a boring, monotone voice to make the eulogy more engaging for the audience.

Creating variations in tone and pace can be hard to do when you are reading from a script, so practising this aspect of delivery is important. Think of speaking about something that you are passionate about or recounting an interesting story to a group of friends. It's that level of interest and variety in your voice that helps to capture people's attention. If you image the sound profile of your voice, try not to be flat and continuous (like the countryside in Holland), but speak with peaks and troughs of tone and pace (like the Alps).

Eye contact

A great way to increase the connection and engagement with the audience is to make brief eye contact as you work through the eulogy. Start at the back of the room to make sure that you are projecting your voice, then make time to look up and connect with people as you work through the script. Glance up at people on each side of the room, the front and at the back. Looking up from the lectern gives you some visual feedback and support from the audience and helps to make tiny individual connections and engagement as you go along. You may find eye contact with a reassuring friend helps to build your confidence.

Talk to individuals you mention

If you are referring to somebody in the building during the eulogy, try and look at the them if you know where they are sitting. Making eye contact helps with voice projection, and watching their reaction hopefully gives some reassurance that you are being heard. Even if you can't locate specific people in the audience, make quick eye contact with people in different areas of the building when you get the chance. Looking around the whole audience helps to make everyone feel they are being included.

Take pauses

It's very tempting to try and get the whole process over and done with rapidly, but take a few pauses to catch your breath. Even a tiny pause lets the audience absorb what you are telling them and creates a useful signpost that you are switching to a new topic.

There is nothing to fear in a couple of seconds silence as you finish a page and turn your notes, it will feel much longer to you than the people listening.

Mark the script for speaking style

A useful way to help remember some of these speaking style tips is to mark up the script to remind you to include them in your delivery. Using a different colour pen, you could include some or all of the following markups as reminders:

- Underline words or phrases that you want to emphasise. This can help with creating interesting tone and variation in pace
- Draw a little pause sign as a reminder to breathe or take a moment to let your words sink in
- Use a little eyeball symbol every now and again to remind you to lift your head and look around the room

Adding your own little marks and reminders after a couple of practise runs is a great way to elevate your delivery from simple reading to giving a eulogy that really connects with the audience.

End of chapter prompts (delivery: speaking style)

Make a check of these points during your practise sessions or recordings:

Prompt	Notes
Can you be heard? Lift your head and project your voice	
Speed: are you talking too quickly to be clearly audible?	
Light and shade: is the tone of your voice varying (Alps) or monotone (Holland)?	
Pauses: are there any obvious places to pause and take breath?	
Eye contact: can you create the mental breathing space to look around the room?	
Mark the script: add cues that will help refine your delivery	

Delivery: physical aspects

Use good posture to your advantage

Speaking in a nice clear voice, creating some light and shade, and making sure you don't go too fast are all extremely important parts of getting your message across. One element that shouldn't be forgotten is how you appear to the audience as you stand in front of them. You want people to focus solely on your voice and message, this chapter provides some tips that can help you avoid any visual distractions that could detract from your delivery.

Stance

Make sure that you stand up tall as you address the audience. Try not to let your nerves make you curl up into a ball, this will make it harder to look up and project your voice into the room. Bringing your shoulders back helps to open up your airway and makes you look confident in front of the audience. If you are practising in front of a mirror or a video camera, use the opportunity to check how your stance looks and correct your posture if necessary.

Try to avoid putting your hand in your pocket, it looks a little too casual for a formal event and can ruin the line of your suit or outfit.

Don't fidget

It's inevitable that you will be nervous to some degree on the day, but try not to let those nerves come across in a physical manifestation. I have seen multiple speeches and talks given by people who create a subconscious outlet for their nervous energy. Often nerves appear through jiggling a leg or shifting from side to side. Sitting in the audience it's easy to become distracted by a visual stimulus, instead of listening to the words. People with long hair can be tempted to fiddle with a stray lock. Often you won't realise you are moving or fiddling, so here are a couple of ways around it:

1. Ask a friend or family member to watch you practise, and gently point out any movements that you are making that you might be unaware of.

2. On the day of the memorial, use your notes to your advantage by placing your hands gently onto either side and keeping them there, removing the temptation to fiddle.

Make use of the lectern

While we are thinking about creating the best physical impression, it is worth knowing whether you will be using a lectern when you are delivering the eulogy. Standing at a lectern can help with keeping your head lifted to project your voice. A lectern also provides a handy place to rest your hands and avoid distracting or nervous movements.

If you won't have a lectern to work with, then pay particular attention to how you hold your notes so that you can keep you head high. I would recommend holding notes at chest height, probably be a little higher than your natural instinct.

Take deep breaths

Taking a couple of slow and deep breaths before you start speaking will help to calm your nerves and heart rate before you start. Use your positive stance (standing tall, shoulders back and head lifted) to calm your breathing and assist with a clear, confident delivery.

When you pause to take a breath, make sure it is full and deep so that you can make it to the end of each sentence in the script without rushing or lowering the volume of your voice.

End of chapter prompts (delivery: physical aspects)

Make a check of these points during your practise sessions or recordings:

Prompt	Notes
Stance – have you got a stance that looks natural and smart?	
Are you making any distracting, subconscious fidgeting movements that can be eliminated?	
Lifting your notes and head – can you project your voice and look at the audience?	
Breathing: take several deep breaths at the start, and breath fully throughout	

Delivery: know the venue

Get to know your surroundings

As the day of the funeral or memorial draws closer, it's natural that the level of nerves will start to rise. I found that a great way to reduce my nerves was to get familiar with the physical surroundings of the funeral venue so that I had a plan of exactly what I would need to do on the day itself.

If you are actively involved in the arrangements of the funeral, it is likely that you will get chance to visit the venue in advance and possibly take part in a rehearsal. It may not be possible to get to the venue in advance of the funeral or memorial, particularly if you live in a different town or country. It is still possible to research details in advance so that you can be as familiar as possible with the location and concentrate more on your delivery.

Research venue size and layout

If you aren't able to visit the venue in person, using an internet search to look for images of the venue should help your preparation. Ideally, look for some detail of the building interior to get an idea of the seating capacity and where you will be standing at the front. Knowing the size and layout of the seating in advance gives you a solid idea of how far you will need to project your voice on the day. Assuming that you will be sitting relatively near to the front, your research will help to visualise the walk up to the lectern on the day of the service. If you are lucky, the venue may have their own website that offers some useful images of the interior.

Venue seating arrangements

Try to get an understanding of the building interior proportions; this can be used to help with your delivery style. If it is very wide with long rows of seats, make a mental note to include the members of the audience at the edges of the seating and addressing each corner of the room. If the building is narrow and long, then the focus should be projecting your voice to back of the space.

Keep your head high and look up from the notes, check for signs that people at the back of the room can hear what you are saying.

Lectern and microphone

Hopefully you will be able to establish in advance if there is a lectern and microphone for you to use on the day. If you can't work this out from rehearsals or research, it would be worth contacting somebody at the venue or the person officiating the service to get some assurance in advance. If there is no lectern, then make sure your practise session includes holding your notes up in front of you.

Dealing with outside venues

It's possible that you may be required to deliver your eulogy in an outdoor environment, depending on the type of service. Use the same sort of preparation that you would undertake to familiarise yourself with a building (knowing the seating layout, if people will be sitting or standing, knowing if you have a lectern and microphone to work with). Pay particular attention to projecting your voice, as it's highly likely there will be additional background noise to overcome.

End of chapter prompts (delivery: know the venue)

Prompt	Notes
Venue size and layout: where will you be speaking from?	
Audience seating arrangements: how will you adapt your delivery?	
Lectern and microphone: is there a lectern to use, will you have a microphone?	
Outside venues or noise: are there any other sources of noise that you may need to adapt to?	

Delivery: timing movements around the venue

Understanding the running order

The final detail that can really help you to feel prepared for delivering a eulogy is knowing the arrangements for the running order of the service. It often won't be the case that there is the opportunity for a full-length rehearsal, so contacting the person officiating the service to get some more detailed timings is a good idea.

The exact details will depend on the type of service (religious or not, cremation or burial etc.) but typically expect to stand up to speak about halfway through the proceedings.

Being prepared means you can engage in the service

Attending a funeral is a significant part of the grieving process, so having the headspace to engage as fully as possible is important. Being prepared on the exact timings of when you need to stand and read the eulogy should allow you to remain calm and focus on what is happening.

Be ready to walk to the lectern

If you know you will be speaking after a specific reading or piece of music, then make sure that you have your notes unfolded, and ready to use before the section finishes. Try and position yourself on the end of a row so that you don't have to push past people to get up to the front of the venue. It doesn't matter if there is a short pause while you make your way up to the front, it will feel like an eternity to you, but it will be just one of many minor logistical pauses in the proceedings.

Watch for trips hazards

If there are any steps or ramps to navigate, plan in your mind's eye how you will safely get to the front of the room to deliver the eulogy. A stumble on the way to the lectern could be unsettling just before you start. If there is opportunity to practise the walk in advance, it would be worth taking it. If you need support or assistance to walk, make sure your helper is briefed on when you need to start moving.

End of chapter prompts (delivery: timing movements around the venue)

Prompt	Notes
Know when you will be required to speak: is there a hymn or reading that precedes your spot on the running order?	
Plan your walk to the lectern: do you need to start walking during the preceding item?	
Trip hazards: do you have a plan to make it safely to the front?	

Afterwards

After the service

After you have navigated your way through delivering the eulogy and the formal parts of the funeral event, in many cases there will be a social gathering to celebrate the life of the deceased. At my own father's funeral, I was surprised by the number of people that approached me to say how much they had enjoyed listening to the eulogy, adding their own anecdotes and memories of my father into the mix. I was approached by lots of people that I had either never met before or hadn't seen for years.

I mention this only because I hadn't thought about it in advance, it was a pleasant surprise and gave me a great sense of pride in the work that I had put into preparing the eulogy.

Have a copy ready to send out

Several people asked me for hard copies of the eulogy to read, or wanted me to send them an electronic version for them to circulate to extended groups of friends or colleagues. It's not critical for the day of the funeral, but preparing a copy that is well formatted and presented could be time well spent so that you are able to send it quickly after the funeral. It may also be worth having a notebook and pencil to hand to jot down the names and details of people that were asking for copies.

Send a copy to people that couldn't make the day

If there is anyone that would have dearly loved to attend the funeral service but couldn't, it would mean a great deal to them if you share a copy of the eulogy with them after the event. If there is a spare copy of the order of service, it may be a nice gesture to include that in the post for them as well. There have been times when I have been out of the country when a funeral has taken place, being able to read the eulogy after the event is a nice way to catch up on what you missed and take some time out to reflect on your loss.

End of chapter prompts (afterwards)

None of these prompts are essential, but may be of use on the day of the funeral service or wake:

Prompt	Notes
Consider preparing spare copies in advance, save a pdf version for sending electronically	
Be ready to capture contact details of people who would like to receive a copy	
Do you need to send copies to people that couldn't attend?	

Wake Ideas

This chapter is entirely unrelated to preparing and giving the eulogy, but I wanted to briefly share a couple of ideas for the wake that helped to make the day go by smoothly when we said goodbye to my father.

Slide show of photographs

If you can organise a computer and a projector screen, having some favourite photographs of your loved one is a super prompt for people to share their memories and recollections. My sister and I took photographs with our phones from hard-copy photograph albums and trawled the various digital repositories of images that we had of my father. I used an online tool to merge the photographs into a video file that I could play on a loop from my PC. This was a time-consuming activity, but relatives in particular were delighted to see some vintage photographs complete with retro fashions and hairstyles in abundance.

Display of favourite possessions / trophies / crafts etc

If there are any favourite items that the deceased was well known for making or wearing or any trophies that they were particularly proud of, then consider bringing them along to the funeral for everyone to see and enjoy. If they are of extremely high sentimental value, then consider the risk of damage and handling very carefully. A well laid out display (even with a "do not touch" sign) would probably be of great interest to people attending the wake.

Music

Playing some of the deceased's favourite music into the wake is a great way to focus on something positive that brought joy into their life. Having a CD or streaming app prepared with a means of playing songs aloud is simple to set up, the wake venue may also be able to assist. It doesn't need to be endlessly on loop, but a quick canter through their favourite style of music, or a couple of their most-listened-to albums will likely raise a smile.

End of chapter prompts (wake preparation)

Prompt	Notes
Photographs: is there a way to display a selection of photographs in the venue of the wake?	
Can you ask somebody to help transport and display some possessions or favourite items?	
Is there somewhere safe to display possessions / items?	
Music: what songs or albums can you compile into a playlist?	

Final thoughts

Nobody wants to be in a position where they need to be writing a eulogy, hopefully the advice in this book will make the process a little easier for you. Having been through the process myself and had a couple of years to reflect on my father's funeral, here are some positive observations that may resonate.

1. The eulogy and funeral are by no means the end of the grieving process, but writing a eulogy helps with acceptance and understanding of what has happened
2. Speaking publicly about how much the person you have lost will be missed is very personal, but seems like a cathartic process after you have done it
3. The eulogy will never be perfect, either in terms of the wording or the delivery. Be happy that you have given it your best effort amongst the constraints of busy modern life and dealing with grief
4. If something goes wrong, don't panic. Despite all the practise you may stumble or cry, or a baby may scream in the audience. Don't feel pressure for everything to be flawless, life happens.

I'd like to express my sympathy for your loss one more time and wish you the best of luck in preparing and delivering your eulogy.

Appendix: Example Eulogy

I have included as an example the eulogy that I wrote for my late father Roger. It's not intended to be a template or to be copied, but I hope it gives a flavour of how the advice contained in this book can be used.

I chose to try and raise a few smiles during the funeral service, you may pick a more formal and factual style. Go with whatever you think is most appropriate and the easiest to deliver on the day.

I have included the topic headings that I used during the writing process to show how I planned the structure and grouped stories together before editing.

My estimate is that this example takes ten minutes to read aloud at a steady pace, this is at the upper limit of what I would recommend for duration. As a rough guidance, it is just under 1,800 words in length.

I have hidden the detail of some dates, names, and locations for the purpose of protecting the personal information of my family. These redactions are marked with XXXX.

If it helps to understand the content a little more, my dad was Roger, my mum is Jean and my sister is Jo/Joanne.

Eulogy – Roger Hartley

Intro

On behalf of our family, I'd like to say thank you for coming today to pay your respects to my dad, Roger. It's a great support to see you all here in person and it means a lot to my mum Jean and our family to have you here with us.

The last time that I was stood at this lectern was 11 years ago, doing a reading on a much happier day – when Joanne and Stewart were married in this church. Roger always loved a large family gathering and often had a few, well-chosen words carefully prepared to celebrate the event. Although today is a very sad gathering of his family and friends, we have prepared a few words in his memory just as he would have done.

Schooling and career

Roger was born in XXXX at the XXXX Hospital in Derby. It was in the period of the Second World War running up to D-Day, and his father Harold was confined to his landing craft in the invasion fleet moored off Lymington. News of Roger's birth was signalled to the ship just before Harold set sail to France.

Harold left the Royal Marines and joined the police force, as a result Roger was raised and schooled all around Derbyshire, with his longest stay at any one school in Glossop during his secondary school years. He studied Geography at Leeds University from 19XX-XX, moving on to complete a teaching diploma in Hull the year after.

Roger started his teaching career in Romford, Essex but soon returned to his Derbyshire roots after taking a post in Belper. His next job was at St. Helena's school in Chesterfield, where he met another teacher that is well known to us all (a certain Jean XXXX). From St. Helena's he moved on to William Rhodes school, becoming Head of Geography and Head of Humanities. In the early nineties my mum and dad ended up teaching together again at Brookfield school, until he took early retirement in XXXX.

So many of his friends and colleagues from his teaching career have sent us lovely cards and letters describing what a dedicated teacher he was, and how much they appreciated him as a supportive and caring colleague.

Although he technically retired in XXXX, he carried on doing supply teaching for several years afterwards, often donning his PE kit despite being well into his fifties.

Marriage to Jean

My mum and dad enjoyed life to the full together, Jo and I were pulling together photographs for the wake and we were struck by how many amazing trips and adventures they took together.

Although he was never a great romantic, actions always spoke louder than words with Roger. Simple gestures, like spoiling my mum with breakfast in bed at the weekends for years, were the clue about just how much he loved Jean. He provided unwavering support for her over the years, not least after her stroke in more recent times when he excelled as her all-action carer.

Derbyshire

Roger always loved the history and topography of Derbyshire, and I'm sure many of you will recognise the Derbyshire flag that we have chosen to use for him today. He was a Peak District Ranger for 17 years, stationed across the park at Langsett House, Tissington, Monsal Head, Hartingdon, Tideswell and Stanedge. He was often accompanied on assignments by Jean in the early years, prior to the arrival of yours truly.

His love of the Peak District was always evident on days out together, it seemed as though there was no footpath, track, tiny lane or indeed country pub that he didn't know like the back of his hand. We have many happy memories of family hikes in the park, with lots of tired legs as a result. After several hours on the march, we always seemed to be either 'just one more field' away or 'very nearly there' when it came to getting back to the car.

Walking Achievements

Roger's love of walking wasn't just confined to Derbyshire, he walked extensively all over the UK. He completed most of the national walking trails including the Pennine Way with his brother Ian, and the Coast-to-Coast path. He climbed all 211 Wainwright peaks in the Lake District and all 53 '2,000 footers' in Snowdonia (completing his mountain leadership certificate in the process).

Even in retirement the achievements kept coming, visiting all 39 English county tops with Jean. He also trekked in the Alps and Pyrenees, staying in mountain refuges and using the 'via farrata' (or iron paths) on some seriously vertiginous ascents.

He has passed down a love of the outdoors to his family, and certainly within my own Hartley household the tradition of over-ambitious family hikes lives on strongly.

Sporting Prowess

Roger was a keen sportsman, particularly in his younger years when his knees still worked properly. He was a good cricketer, and played for Bakewell, Cromford Meadows and the Chesterfield Barbarians. His distinctive left-handed bowling style was particularly effective against the opposition.

Many of his teaching colleagues have remarked upon his commitment to sport at school, including inter-department games and staff/student matches. There was a famous football match against students (that the staff won) where my dad proudly worked out the combined age of the back four was over 200 years.

More recently he loved his crown-green bowling and was a proud member of Wingerworth Bowling Club. He enjoyed travelling out to away matches and achieved plenty of home success with his partners Graham and Peter.

At family get-togethers there was often a competitive element, there are many happy memories of fierce croquet matches being played in the back garden.

Food and Garden

It was in the garden that he focused huge amounts of his energy, he loved a landscaping project, and was a keen grower of vegetables in his greenhouse. He had a unique form of greenhouse pest control, the smoke from a secret hamlet cigar seemed to be surprisingly effective against greenfly!

The outputs from his vegetable patch were always turned into a variety of homemade treats. His green tomato chutney, pickled onions and piccalilli were the stuff of legend, frequently gifted to friends and family. His Saturday morning fry-ups and his ability to whip up a picnic for eight people in under five minutes will also be sorely missed. Not to mention his rocket fuel-strength gin and tonics.

He was also a creature of habit with meals; lunch was always at 12:45 and dinner was always at 17:45 sharp. In the eighties this caused a major problem for Jo and me, as Neighbours started at 17:35 and finished at 18:00! Eventually we managed to push family dinner time to 18:00, until we both left home at least.

Home brew beer was also another favourite gastronomic pastime for my dad, with barrels stashed in the airing cupboard and rows of bottles stacked up in the garage. It was the day after a new white kitchen had been fitted at home that he decided to open a particularly lively bottle over the sink. It exploded in a giant fountain, all over the whole room. After hearing the blast my mum rushed in to find him frantically mopping beer off the ceiling with a tea towel.

Total commitment

Roger never started on a task or a project without giving 100% commitment to undertaking it thoroughly and seeing it through to completion. Just looking at the garden in their new house is an amazing testament to his work ethic, from rubble to completed in under six months.

Perhaps most notable was his focus on family history during his retirement. He documented in incredible detail the family tree and histories of the XXXX family, and Jean's side of the tree as well.

He loved the process of undertaking research and finding and meeting extended family members across the country.

Technology

Although Roger did grapple with the internet and computing for the family histories, he never did really master the art of technology – especially the mobile phone. Though he did have a phone for many years, it was always either off or had been left at home when you needed him.

For many years Roger attended a quiz at The Grouse pub with his good friend Nigel. Arrangements for meeting would run as follows: around 5pm on Wednesdays my dad would turn on his phone. A text message would come in from Nigel, containing a single '?'. My dad would simply reply with a 'Y' if he could make it, or an 'N' if not. Simple and effective man-to-man communication.

Generous with time

As I'm sure everyone here knows, Roger was often a man of few words. How he really showed his care and commitment was with the generous donation of his time and effort. To his own family that manifested itself in the creation of incredible homemade toys, to others it was time spent helping in the house and garden.

He devoted many days and hours to helping Jo and me with our new house projects, often helping to look after grandchildren at the same time. If Roger was staying during the week, there was trouble if you returned home from work and the list of jobs that was left in the morning had not been sufficient to occupy him all day.

Omelette / Eggs

Much as we loved the frenetic pace at which many of these jobs would be undertaken and completed, if there was ever a man that the phrase 'you can't make an omelette without breaking eggs' was invented for, it was Roger. He permanently had either a black thumbnail or toenail from hitting them with a hammer / spade / brick / axe / chisel (delete as appropriate).

Although his head never had much hair on it, it was covered with cuts and scars from being constantly bashed into the car boot, greenhouse doorframe or loft-hatch opening. None of these injuries ever slowed him down, they were just a minor inconvenience on the path to completion.

Summary

So, to conclude, it's with a lot of sadness but also a lifetime of happy memories that we celebrate the life of Roger today. He was a multi-talented teacher, Ranger, expedition leader, sportsman, gardener, builder, chef, genealogist and carer. On top of all of that, he was a loving father who doted on his family.

He's left behind a legacy that we are all hugely proud of. Not just a physical legacy in the Peak District and gardens around the country, but a legacy of learning for the hundreds of pupils that he taught over the years.

And most importantly to us, a legacy of his values, his humour and his kindness that will live on with all of us for years to come.

We will miss you Grandpa.

Author Profile

David Hartley lost his father to cancer in 2021, he wanted to give the best possible eulogy at the funeral but found advice on the subject was limited to basic writing tips. He resolved to write a comprehensive guide on how to plan, write and deliver a eulogy to share with people experiencing their own loss.

David is a mechanical engineer and project management professional; he shares his insight into public speaking and presenting to large audiences in this book.

Outside of writing and projects, David runs a stationery company (see more at www.leafgraphpaper.com) and is delighted to give the tasks of printing and distributing to others for the first time.

Away from work, David loves all things related to the outdoors and waterways and is never happier then when cruising a river on his paddleboard.